My Fantastic VACATION Journal

A Fun Fill-in Book for Kids

Diana Zourelias

Dover Publications, Inc.
Mineola, New York

W9-BZP-648

My Name: _____

Our Destination: _____

Trip Dates: _____

Copyright

Copyright © 2019 by Diana Zourelias
All rights reserved.

Bibliographical Note

My Fantastic Vacation Journal is a new work, first published
by Dover Publications, Inc. in 2019.

International Standard Book Number

ISBN-13: 978-0-486-82415-4
ISBN-10: 0-486-82415-2

Manufactured in the United States by LSC Communications
82415201   2019
www.doverpublications.com

NOTE

Wherever you're headed on vacation, this is really the only carry-on item you need! Packed with page after page of comical illustrations and fun fill-ins, you'll have a great time writing, drawing, and doodling about your travels. From creating a cute suitcase sticker and original T-shirt design to listing favorite new foods you've tried and recording addresses of new friends you've made, the huge variety of activities will keep you entertained along the way. And when you get back home, this journal will be a cool keepsake that will help you to remember how much fun you had on your trip.

I'm going on Vacation with:

O 1. My Family_____
  _____

O 2. A School Group___
  _____

O 3. A Social Group___
  _____

O 4. A Relative _____
  _____

O 5. My Friend's Family
  _____

O 6. My Dog_____
  _____

O 7. Other _____
  _____

Check One

1

I will be on Vacation for:

A. A Weekend
B. A Week
C. 2 Weeks
D. Other _____

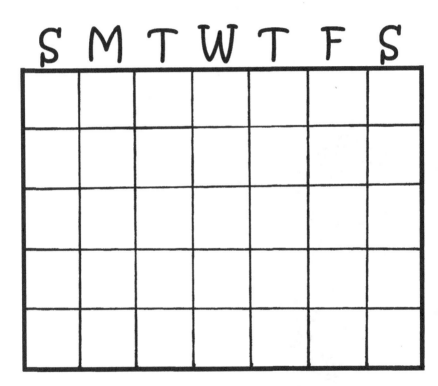

S	M	T	W	T	F	S

Fill in the Dates of Your Calendar

I will be Traveling by:

- ☐ 1. Car
- ☐ 2. Bus
- ☐ 3. Plane
- ☐ 4. Cruise Ship
- ☐ 5. Train

- ☐ 6. RV
- ☐ 7. Bike
- ☐ 8. Helicopter
- ☐ 9. Spaceship
- ☐ 10. Other _____

Check One

My Favorite Place to sit in the Car (Plane, Bus, Train, Boat) is _____

_____

_____

My Least Favorite seat is ___

_____

Because _____

_____

_____

_____

4

These are some of the Activities I am Looking Forward to Doing on Vacation:

- ☐ A. Sleeping
- ☐ B. Staying up Late
- ☐ C. Endless Time on my Tablet
- ☐ D. Inside Sports
- ☐ E. Outside Sports
- ☐ F. Meeting New People
- ☐ G. Seeing New Places
- ☐ H. Trying Different Foods
- ☐ I. Being Away from _____
- ☐ J. _____

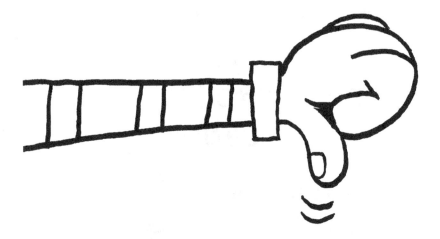

I am/am NOT Looking
Forward to my Vacation
because _____

_____
_____
_____
_____
_____
_____
_____
_____

My Favorite part of Traveling is

_____
_____
_____
_____

My Least Favorite part is _____

_____
_____
_____
_____

I would NEVER leave Home
without _____

_____

_____

Because _____

_____

_____

_____

_____

If I could pick ANYWHERE in the WORLD to VACATION it would be

_____

_____

_____

_____

Because _____

_____

_____

_____

_____

_____

9

I have Visited many Interesting Places. This is a List of my Favorites.

Places

Description

_____   _____

_____   _____

_____   _____

_____   _____

_____   _____

_____   _____

_____   _____

_____   _____

Places   Description

Places	Description
_____	_____
_____	_____
_____	_____
_____	_____
_____	_____
_____	_____
_____	_____
_____	_____
_____	_____

If I could choose Famous People to Travel with, I would pick

_____

Because _____

The One Person I keep in Touch with while Traveling is _____

_____

_____

_____

Because _____

_____

_____

_____

_____

There's always a chance you'll get something Annoying while on a Trip. I'm Afraid of...

Sunburn   Bug Bites   Sand in Pants
Frostbite   Cold   Allergies
Duck Bite   Poison Ivy   Diaper Rash
Windburn   Sore Feet   Wart
Cut or Bruise   Sty   Ingrown Toenail
Food Poisoning   Black Eye   Dandruff
Tapeworm   Toothache   Other

Circle All that apply

I hope to have some of my Favorite
Snacks while I'm away and maybe
try some New Ones too!

OLD
Favorites

NEW
Favorites

OLD Favorites	NEW Favorites
_____	_____
_____	_____
_____	_____
_____	_____
_____	_____
_____	_____
_____	_____
_____	_____

When I close my eyes and think about my **Vacation**, some of these **Smells** come to mind:

☐ Grilled Food   ☐ Coconut
☐ Ocean and Seashells
☐ Cotton Candy   ☐ Suntan Lotion
☐ Hot Dogs   ☐ Hot Chocolate
☐ Feet   ☐ Other _____

While looking out of the Window,
I saw some Interesting Clouds.
Here's a drawing of my Favorite One!

Decorate the Travel Stickers on this Suitcase

Design Original License Plates for a Favorite State or Country you Recently Visited.

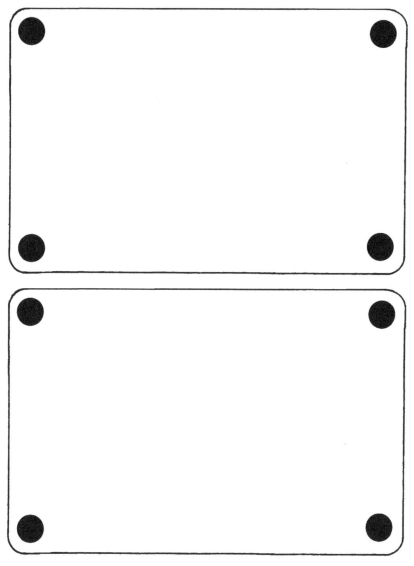

Make as Many Words as you Can out of the Word

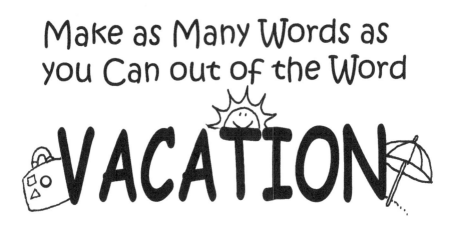

VACATION

_____ _____

_____ _____

_____ _____

_____ _____

_____ _____

_____ _____

_____ _____

_____ _____

_____ _____

_____ _____

Vacations are usually very busy and you don't get much rest! When I get Home, I'm going to sleep for _____

Hours or More!

DOODLE PAGE

I get Sooo Bored waiting around on Vacation...

☆ DOODLE PAGE ☆

Glad I have these Doodle Pages!

Play I Spy! with your Travel Mates!

I Spy with My Little Eye!

List: _____

_____

_____

_____

_____

_____

_____

_____

_____

TRAVEL JOKE CHALLENGE

Match each Joke on THIS Page to its Punch Line on the Opposite Page.

1. How can you tell that Elephants love to Travel?
2. Why did the Witch stay in a Hotel?
3. Where do Sheep go on Vacation?
4. Where do Sharks go on Vacation?
5. Where do Hamsters go on Vacation?
6. What do Frogs like to Drink on a Hot Summer's Day?
7. How do Rabbits get to their Holiday Destination?
8. What did the Pig say on the Beach?
9. What travels around the World but stays in one Corner?
10. What do you get when you cross an Airplane with a Magician?
11. Where do Cows go on Vacation?
12. Where do Cows like to go in the Evenings?
13. What did the Pacific Ocean say to the Atlantic Ocean?
14. What is a Vampire's Favorite Airline?
15. What Happens when you Wear a Watch on a plane?

A. Nothing, it just Waved.
B. By Hare-Plane.
C. They always pack their own Trunk!
D. To the Mooooo-vies!
E. Hamsterdam!
F. A Stamp!
G. Moo York!
H. The Baaa-hamas!
I. Scare Canada!
J. Finland!
K. I'm Bacon!
L. Time Flies!
M. A Flying Sorcerer
N. She heard they had Great Broom Service!
O. Croak-a-Cola

Write your own Joke. _____

_____

_____

_____

Attach a Photo
from your Trip
HERE.

Attach a Photo
from your Trip
HERE.
Draw a Frame
around it.

If I could wish for One Thing
to be Different on My
Vacation, it would be

_____

_____

_____

_____

_____

_____

_____

If I could pick Cartoon Characters
as my Travel Companions, I would
choose _____

_____

_____

_____

_____

_____

_____

I left Home at:

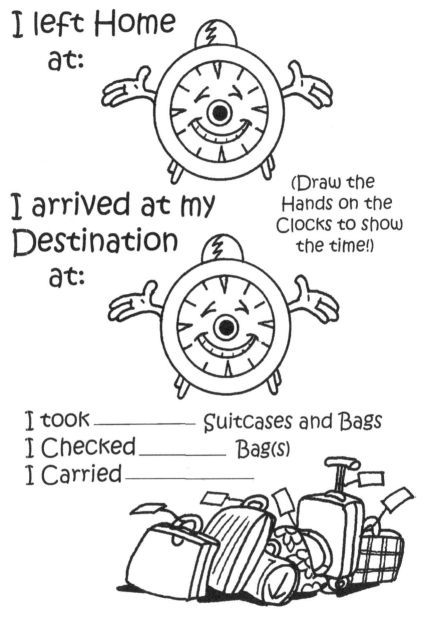

(Draw the Hands on the Clocks to show the time!)

I arrived at my Destination at:

I took _____ Suitcases and Bags
I Checked _____ Bag(s)
I Carried _____

Finally HOME!

Date: _____

Time: _____

I Felt: _____

☐ 1. Happy   ☐ 5. Tired

☐ 2. Sad   ☐ 6. Hungry

☐ 3. Relieved   ☐ 7. Overjoyed

☐ 4. Nervous   ☐ 8. Other_____

Of all the Vacations I've been on, here are my Rankings for This One.

1-10 (1 for Worst, 10 for Best Ever!)

- ☐ Food
- ☐ Transportation
- ☐ Interesting things to See and Do
- ☐ People I met
- ☐ Weather
- ☐ Expenses
- ☐ Fun
- ☐ Comfort

HMMM

I'd give this Trip a Score
of _____ out of 10
Because _____

_____

_____

_____

_____

_____

_____

If I had to write a Book or Story about this Vacation, the Title would be:

by

Here are 5 Words to Describe This Trip:

1. _____

2. _____

3. _____

4. _____

5. _____

If I had to Choose just one, it would be ____

_____

FABULOUS

LONG   DUMB

TIRING   BEST

SUNNY RAINY Partly Cloudy LIGHTNING

The WEATHER for Most of the Trip was _____

_____

The WORST was _____

_____

The BEST was _____

_____

HAIL WINDY SLEET

PARTLY SUNNY

RAINBOW

ICY
BRRR!

WEATHER CHART

This is a Drawing of the Expression on my Face if I were told I will be going to this Destination again

Next Year!

This is the Funniest thing
that Happened on my
Vacation! (Made me LOL!)

My Most Favorite Meal on Vacation Looked like This!

My Least Favorite Meal
on Vacation Looked Like
This!

Here's a Drawing
of a Souvenir I
took Home!
I got it at _____
_____
_____

One thing that was sooo Boring
it made me Yawn! (and still makes
me yawn thinking about it!)

_____

_____

_____

_____

_____

_____

This is what I read on Vacation

Reading List: _____

_____

_____

_____

_____

_____

_____

_____

_____

My Favorite: _____

It was about _____

_____

I Always forget something at Home! This time it was

_____

and I had to use _____
_____ instead.

The Coolest thing I did on this Trip was —————————————————

——————————————————————

Because ————————————————

——————————————————————

——————————————————————

——————————————————————

——————————————————————

——————————————————————

A TV Show about my Vacation would be called:

_____

It would be a:

1. Drama
2. Kids' Show
3. Comedy
4. Talk Show
5. Sports Show

6. Reality Show
7. Game Show
8. Other_____

(Circle One)

The BEST Place I ate on Vacation was

_____

I ordered _____

_____

The WORST Place I ate was_____

I ordered _____

_____

_____

This is the Best Joke I heard on Vacation:_____

_____

_____

_____

_____

_____

_____

_____

_____

_____

If I had to design a
T-Shirt
to remind me of
This Trip,
it would look like this.

On my Vacation I Slept...

(Check all that apply)

- ☐ In a HUGE Bed
- ☐ In a tiny Bed
- ☐ In a Bunk Bed
- ☐ In a Comfy Chair
- ☐ In a Not-So-Comfy Chair
- ☐ In a Sleeping Bag
- ☐ In an RV
- ☐ In a Hammock
- ☐ In a Tent
- ☐ On an Inflatable Bed
- ☐ In a Car
- ☐ Outdoors under the Stars
- ☐ Other _____

It was BETTER/WORSE than where I Sleep at Home Because _____

The Biggest Lesson I learned on
this trip was _____

_____

_____

Because _____

_____

_____

_____

_____

I saw these Movies on my Trip:

My Fave was _____

_____

Because _____

_____

_____

I tried this New Food for the First Time on this Trip:

_____

☐ I liked it!
☐ I DIDN'T Like it.

Because _____
_____
_____
_____
_____
_____
_____

It's Always nice to
Get Back HOME!
These are the Things that Changed while I was Away:

_____

_____

_____

_____

These stayed the Same: _____

_____

_____

_____

The First thing I did when I got Home was:

A. Sleep
B. Cry
C. Shower
D. Pet the Dog, Cat, Hamster, Fish, Bird
E. Jump up and down for Joy
F. Binge-watch all the Shows I missed
G. Eat a Snack
H. Race to the Bathroom

I Got to Stay at:

- ☐ Hotel
- ☐ Motel
- ☐ Ski Lodge
- ☐ Campgrounds
- ☐ Relatives' House
- ☐ Haunted House
- ☐ Tree House
- ☐ Igloo
- ☐ Castle
- ☐ Resort
- ☐ Other_____

Which was:

- ☐ Huge
- ☐ Cold
- ☐ Quiet
- ☐ Fancy
- ☐ Scary
- ☐ Fun
- ☐ Wet
- ☐ Crowded
- ☐ Stinky
- ☐ Buggy

I saw a plane skywriting,
and it wrote _____

_____

_____

_____

If I were a pilot, I would
write _____

_____

_____

_____

_____

One Person from this Trip
I will Always Remember is

_____

_____

Because_____

_____

_____

The First Person I called (e-mailed, texted) when I got home was

_____

I couldn't wait to tell him/her about

_____
_____
_____
_____

Sometimes it's Scary when you do something NEW! This is what scared me the MOST!

_____

_____

_____

Because_____

_____

_____

_____

_____

If I could have Traveled to my Vacation Destination in a Different Vehicle, I would have Chosen:

1. Air Force One
2. Unicycle
3. Transporter
4. Space Shuttle
5. Limo
6. Elephant
7. Helicopter
8. Rickshaw
9. Pirate Ship
10. Dogsled
11. Submarine
12. Santa's Sleigh
13. Flying Carpet
14. Other _____

The Most
Annoying
Person
I met was

_____
_____
_____
_____

She/He annoyed me
because _____

_____
_____
_____
_____
_____

One Disappointing thing about this
Vacation was _____

_____

_____

_____

_____

Because ———————————————

_____

_____

_____

_____

_____

Sometimes Teachers ask you to write an Essay about your Vacation. Here are some Highlights, so I won't Forget!

The one thing I REALLY wanted to do but DIDN'T was...

SIGH...

_____
_____
_____
_____
_____
_____
_____

Because _____
_____
_____
_____
_____
_____

I hate when This happens!

One thing I Lost/Broke on Vacation was _____

And I think it Happened when

_____
_____
_____

I decided to
Splurge
on ONE THING!

It was SO Worth
it Because _____

_____

_____

_____

It was so NOT worth it
Because _____

_____

_____

_____

_____

And here's what that One Thing looks like!

I should've left These
Clothes at Home _____
_____
_____
_____

and Brought these clothes
instead_____
_____
_____
_____

Because _____
_____

There comes a Point in Every Vacation when you just want to Go Home!

_____
_____
_____

For me it Happened on _____ (date) Because ____

_____
_____
_____
_____
_____
_____

Here's a list of some of the Unusual Things I saw on Vacation.

_____   _____

_____   _____

_____   _____

_____   _____

_____   _____

_____   _____

_____   _____

_____   _____

I KNOW you aren't supposed to Stare! (It's Rude!) But when I saw THIS, I couldn't Look Away!

_____

_____

_____

_____

_____

_____

_____

_____

_____

Unlike when I'm Home,
I had no time to _____

_____

_____

_____

while I was away!

Some Things I did on Vacation that Tired Me Out!!! _____

_____

_____

_____

_____

_____

_____

_____

Names of Famous People I met or saw on my Vacation: _____

_____

_____

_____

_____

_____

_____

_____

_____

_____

People I saw on my Vacation who Looked like Famous People:____

_____

_____

_____

_____

_____

_____

_____

_____

Draw a Picture of your Memory

The One Thing that I Close my Eyes and try to Relive is

_____

_____

_____

_____

_____

My friends would be so Jealous
I _____

_____

on Vacation Because _____
_____!

They will NOT be Jealous that I
had to _____

_____!

The ONE Thing missing on this Vacation that would've made it BETTER was _____

_____

Because _____

_____

_____

_____

_____

I took some
FUN
PICTURES
on this
TRIP!

I Wish I had taken one
of This!

I'm starting a List of Places
I've been on Vacation. (This
includes Overnights at Grandma's,
BF's House, Camp, etc.)

PLACE:_____

_____

HOW LONG:_____

_____

WITH WHOM:_____

_____

DATE: _____
MEMORY: _____

_____

_____

PLACE:_____

HOW LONG:_____

WITH WHOM:_____

DATE: _____
MEMORY: _____

_____

PLACE:_____

HOW LONG:_____

WITH WHOM:_____

DATE: _____
MEMORY: _____

_____

_____

_____

Meeting NEW PEOPLE is Fun!
Some of My NEW FRIENDS'
Names and Addresses are:

Name: _____
Address:_____
_____
Phone:_____
E-Mail:_____
What I Like about them:_____
_____
Name:_____
Address:_____
_____
Phone:_____
E-Mail:_____
What I Like about them:_____
_____

Name:_____
Address:_____
_____
Phone:_____
E-mail:_____
What I like about them:_____
_____

Name:_____
Address:_____
_____
Phone:_____
E-mail:_____
What I Like about them:_____
_____

Name:_____
Address:_____
_____
Phone: _____
E-mail:_____
What I Like about them:___
_____

Name:_____
Address:_____
_____
Phone:_____
E-mail:_____
What I like about them:_____
_____

Name:_____
Address:_____
_____
Phone:_____
E-mail:_____
What I Like about them:_____
_____

Name:_____
Address:_____
_____
Phone:_____
E-mail:_____
What I Like about them:____
_____

Name:_____
Address:_____
_____
Phone:_____
E-mail:_____
What I like about them:_____
_____

Name:_____
Address:_____
_____
Phone:_____
E-mail:_____
What I Like about them:_____
_____

Name:_____
Address:_____
_____
Phone: _____
E-mail:_____
What I Like about them:____
_____

Name:_____
Address:_____
_____
Phone:_____
E-mail:_____
What I like about them:_____
_____

Name:_____
Address:_____
_____
Phone:_____
E-mail:_____
What I Like about them:_____
_____

Name:_____
Address:_____
_____
Phone:_____
E-mail:_____
What I Like about them:____
_____